Purpose used to haunt me constantly. What if I could never again do the things I loved to do? What if chronic illness permanently ripped away and erased my old self? What if I can't ever support myself? What do I do then? What future is there for someone like me? What meaning is there in fighting so hard each and every day? *What is my purpose?* What I've discovered is that meaning is an inherent part of being alive, it's the way you choose to live your life. We were created by the God who created everything and that has got to mean something. That's why you're here after all, isn't it? Because you or someone you know is in this place, fighting this fight? **Finding Purpose** doesn't have all the answers, but it is the first step on a journey that will change your life as you rediscover what it means to live a life with chronic illness.

SAM RE, Chronic Illness Warrior

It sounds cliché, but God spoke to me through the pages of **Finding Purpose**. As I read each chapter, I was called to go deeper in Christ and to seek God's true purpose for my life — what a humbling gift to know that although I'm still facing health challenges, I am loved and called by God for a specific purpose. My life is not over yet! To quote Cindee, "I chose God and it made all the difference." I am choosing Him daily as I find His purpose in my life. To God be the glory!

GINA M. WEEKS

Girl, you have done it again! You spoke straight to my heart and the hearts of those who live with chronic illness. Anointed! *You are anointed!* I am so blessed to know you and so honored to walk beside you as you do the hard work and God blesses your obedience. You are amazing. God is amazing! I might have cried a few times too. But I feel so much more encouraged myself just reading through the content of **Finding Purpose**. May the Lord bless all who find it, and may many find it. Such a necessary word of encouragement.

KELLY GREER

Finding Purpose helped me to align my purpose with the purpose that God has for my life. It helped me to realize that everything happens for a reason. Having an illness doesn't mean that God doesn't love you. It means that He has a deeper purpose for your life. Cindee walks you through finding your purpose while she shares stories that connect with each of the chapters. I really enjoyed this book and I am so excited to be able to share it with my family and friends!

JENNIFER RADDATZ

Cindee Snider Re has a heart for the hurting. Because of her own chronic health issues, she has allowed God to use her in a mighty way. As was **Discovering Hope** (the first book in this series), **Finding Purpose** is strongly encouraging. I hope you read it, then encourage another who needs it to read it too.

DIANE McELWAIN

There's nothing out there like **Finding Purpose**. I've often felt other Bible studies were too preachy. Somehow they made me feel that I wasn't enough, and their words were my only hope for salvation. Not this one. **Finding Purpose** helped me realize that God doesn't want us to walk through any part of life alone. It helped me gather what I need within myself to listen to Him, and look for Him in everything. It wasn't written by a stuffy sounding know-it-all, it was written by a kind- hearted friend of everyone.

JEAN B.ELLISON

A sense of intimacy hums on **Finding Purpose**'s pages — intimacy between reader and author, author and God, God and reader. As touching personal, parenting or marriage moments are bravely and vulnerably shared, the reader is spurred to scour and search Scripture for answers to implied and posed questions. The written words open doors and soften hearts, directing the reader straight into the presence of God.

JAN VANKOOTEN

Once again, Cindee has written a book that will get right to the heart for anyone living with chronic illness. **Finding Purpose** has a true Spirit-led motivation that will bring encouragement to those who may have felt there could be no purpose left for them after an unsettling and life-changing diagnosis. The chapters on writing your own allegory and asking God for His life's purpose for you brought rays of beauty into my own dull and grey days with chronic illness. Thank you for sharing these God-given words.

BETTIE GILBERT

You hold in your hands a unique invitation. An invitation to be still with your soul, to lean into Christ, to explore deeply and to emerge full of your true self. **Finding Purpose** brings to light the gift of our lives and our calling. The intimacy of God's presence shines brightly amongst the darkness of chronic illness as we explore and understand our purpose and the power of our presence.

RACHEL THIEL, DPT, OS

Finding Purpose will help you push through chronic illness as a defining destiny, gloriously refining you through the living Word of God. Cindee's personal journey has redefined her life purpose: "to hold hope, seek beauty, chase light and dance with words, because that is how [she] experiences the presence of God, and speaks life into a broken, hurting world."

MARY ELIZABETH CASEY

Finding Purpose

©2017 by Cindee Snider Re
Published by Chronic Joy Ministry, Inc. Waukesha, WI 53188
chronic-joy.org

First Edition: October, 2017
Printed in the United States of America
ISBN: 978-0-9978099-1-6

Cover Image and Interior Design: **kylecreative.com**
Cover Model: **Samantha Abbate**
Author Photo: **Wayde Peronto** of **Babboni Photography**
Subtitle: **Sam Re**
End of Chapter Prayers: **Julie Sheridan Smith**

Printed by CreateSpace

CHRONIC JOY THRIVE SERIES – BOOK 2

Chronic Joy Ministry, Inc.
Radical hope. Compassionate change.
Equipping those affected by chronic physical and mental illness
through community and education rooted in Jesus Christ

Finding Purpose

Rediscovering Meaning in a Life with Chronic Illness

Cindee Snider Re

Chronic Joy Thrive Series
Book 2

Chronic Joy Ministry, Inc.
Waukesha, Wisconsin

To my parents, Don and Susie Snider:

I have always known that I belong. Thank you.

You taught me to see.

Long before I could read, you opened my world to books,
placed a pencil in my hand and fostered a love for language.

Words are where I breathe and feel my heart beat,
where I seek hope and discover meaning,
and often where I encounter Christ.

This book is for you.

Dear Heavenly Father

Finding Purpose is lovingly dedicated to You for Your purposes. May it bring glory and honor to Your name.

Guide those who step into these pages into a closer relationship with You, the author of purpose, and flood their hearts with love, grace, hope and meaning.

Amen.

Pamela K. Piquette
President and Co-Founder, Chronic Joy Ministry, Inc.

Chronic Joy Ministry, Inc.

Chronic Joy Ministry, Inc. was founded to raise awareness of the nearly 1 in 2 people who live with chronic physical and mental illness and its impact on every aspect of life — faith, family, finances, friendships, marriage, education, hobbies and work.

Chronic illness *is* hard, but there *is hope.*

On January 1, 2016, I woke with a vision too big to believe. God broke my heart for the millions — yes, *millions* of people! — living daily with chronic illness, and also for the *one* utterly without hope.

In April 2016, we officially became a 501(c)(3) nonprofit, no small accomplishment, but God was just getting started.

Today, Chronic Joy Ministry offers daily encouragement across social media, has a growing website filled with educational resources and weekly guest blogs, publishes a monthly *Invitation to Prayer* and a quarterly newsletter, and has published the first two books in our four-book study series.

Chronic Joy is a ministry led by God and His word. Luke 15:8-9 speaks to our purpose:

> *Or suppose a woman has ten silver coins and loses one. Doesn't she light a lamp, sweep the house and search carefully until she finds it? And when she finds it, she calls her friends and neighbors together and says, "Rejoice with me; I have found my lost coin.*

This woman had *hope* that she would find her lost coin. She had *purpose* as she searched for what was lost. From the beginning, she knew the intrinsic *worth* of a single coin. And when she found her one lost coin, she experienced such *joy.*

Those are the first four books in our study series: *Discovering Hope, Finding Purpose, Embracing Worth* and *Encountering Joy.* But they are more than titles — they are an invitation to live life with our eyes focused on God, for when we choose Him, He will compassionately change our hearts and lead us to radical hope, rediscovered purpose, eternal worth, and exquisite joy.

Pamela K. Piquette
President and Co-Founder, Chronic Joy Ministry, Inc

PAMELA is a leader and a visionary following God's call to inspire those affected by chronic illness to discover hope, find purpose, embrace worth and encounter joy. She believes every precious life affected by chronic illness is both vital and purposed.

Pamela is a mom of three adult children, grandma of two sweet granddaughters, and a wife of more than 30 years. She is diagnosed with Ehlers-Danlos, chronic migraines and host of other chronic conditions.

Pamela enjoys hot tea, reading – almost always more than one book at a time – and walking her teddy bear dog, Cocoa.

Where do we begin?
Begin with the heart.

Julian of Norwich

Contents

We need words on dark days.

Megan Willome

Foreword

On the day I wrote this Foreword, I was in bed. We'd had to leave church early ... *again*. I was feeling like a failure and figured the most spiritual thing I could do was take a nap. So I did. When I woke up, I made a cup of tea and began looking back over the notes I had made while reading *Finding Purpose*.

Unlike Cindee, I'm not someone who experiences chronic illness, but I might fall into the category of chronic loss. I don't claim it's the same thing. But I do know that this study and the one before it, *Discovering Hope*, have spoken to me in ways that few other Christian resources have in recent years.

As someone who has read the Bible nearly every day since I accepted Jesus into my heart as a child, I hear certain verses a lot — the standards, the greatest hits, those on everyone's Top 10 lists. They're cited for multiple situations, often with a "You go, girl!" spin, which isn't helpful when dealing with chronic illness. Or chronic pain. Or loss. Or grief. That's when those verses start to feel flat. How do I embrace Jeremiah 29:11 when life takes a hard left turn with no hope of getting back on the interstate?

But when Cindee pulled out that verse — and quite a few others on my *Never Again* list — she helped me see them with new eyes. She invited me to remember my life's purpose before everything changed and to consider what it might look like in this new after. "Yes, those verses are still for you," she seems to say.

The chapter on *Purpose: Writing a Biblical Purpose Statement* is the kind of activity I usually avoid. I once told my husband something remarkably like what Cindee told hers: "Dreams weren't meant for someone like me." But then she walks us through seven verses to prepare us to write a Purpose Statement. Since I'd gotten a lot out of writing a lament in her previous study, I was game to try writing this too. So I read, journaled, and let it all sit overnight. To rise.

The next morning — *this morning* — when I had to leave church early and go to bed, I could still read (and write). A comment from my husband led me to revisit a book I'd loved when my son was little, Kenneth Grahame's *The Wind in the Willows*. I journaled about a particular chapter and discovered those notes somehow coinciding with what I'd written the night before about finding purpose. Voila! I had a biblically informed, Wild Wood-inspired, genuine purpose statement.

One that works whether I'm in bed or not. Whether I'm grieving or walking the dogs or praying in the chapel or writing up an interview or reading a poem or choosing which tea will carry me through the day. Even if healing doesn't come. I pray it will do the same for you.

Megan Willome
Author of *The Joy of Poetry*
meganwillome.com

*In the presence of eternity,
the mountains are as transient as the clouds.*

Robert Green Ingersoll

Introduction

My son Sam and I had an interesting conversation the other day. "I know God should be enough," he said, "but sometimes I just need ... no, I want, I guess, a friend, someone to push me, encourage me to work harder, quit slacking off, someone who shares my interests. I don't know, God *should* be enough, and I feel guilty that He's not, but sometimes I just want someone — a person — who gets me."

My response surprised even me. "I'm not sure that's true, that God should be enough," I said. "I mean, He *is* enough, but also think of the Garden of Eden before the Fall. Adam hadn't sinned, so he walked in complete, unbroken relationship with God, and yet God said, 'It's not good for the man to be alone; I'll make him a helper, a companion.' God knew we needed relationship with others. He *knew*, and on purpose, He created Eve so Adam would be complete."

God doesn't expect us to walk this journey alone. He created us in pairs *on purpose*, not because He isn't enough, but because He created us to need one another — not more than we need Him, but together with Him, in Him, through Him. *Together* we are the body of Christ, not each one individual and separate, but *all*, together — not either/or, but both/and.

First God, then community. One Body. Whole. Complete. Every single person necessary.

The genesis of purpose.

We're so glad you're here. We've been praying for you, praying that God would meet you in each word and on every page.

We pray you will rediscover *God's* purpose for your life as you take this next step on your journey through chronic illness.

*The presence of the Holy Spirit is
the keystone of all our hopes.*
John Nelson Darby

Presence

It was 8:05 p.m. on Memorial Day. I was on the freeway with two of my five kids — the oldest and the youngest. The oldest was listening to music. The youngest was watching cars go by her window, announcing indignantly, "Speeder. Speeeeder. Definitely a speeder! Mom, do motorcycles have to go the speed limit too or do they get a free pass?"

I laughed. "No free passes. Motorcycles have to obey the speed limit too."

"Double speeder!" Pause. "Mom?"

"Yeah, Honey?"

"Why is everyone in such a hurry? Can't they just slow down? Where are they all going in such a rush?"

Good questions. Where *are* we all going in such a hurry? Why do we feel the need to rush from one thing to the next without regard for the speed limit, our health, our safety or our lives? Living at such a pace, we fail to live in the moment. We miss the laughter, beauty and joy in our midst, trading them for stress, frustration, anxiety and anger. We forge ahead consumed with the destination while missing the journey. In a sense, we're taking God's precious gift of presence and telling Him it isn't what we want, that we don't have the time.

A few weeks ago, I was on the back of a Harley riding through Alaska. The mountains rose 50 feet from one side of the road and the ocean fell away 100 feet from the other. An eagle soared overhead. Snow capped the peaks and descended into valleys. Icebergs floated in the bay. As we rode through this rugged country, I felt closer to God than I had in months and my daughter's questions surfaced in my mind.

Why *are* we in such a rush? Where are we going in such a hurry? Why do we wait and hope and plan for tomorrow or next week or next year before we slow down and enjoy our lives?

Life isn't awaiting us at a destination, it's happening *right now* and we're missing it.

"Lord," I prayed, "I'm in Alaska, on the back of a Harley, behind the man I love most in this world, and I don't want to miss a minute. Teach me to slow down and experience the immensity of who You are, to be fully present, and savor the gift of time. Teach me to laugh easily, love abundantly, and be content no matter where I am, for I'm beginning to understand that the only way to taste and see just how good You are is to experience life in the slow lane, deeply, richly, fully present every step of the way."

STEPPING IN:

1. Where do you feel rushed today?

2. Read **Psalm 16:11** and fill in the blanks:

    You make known to me the _____ of life; you will

    _____ me with _____ in your presence, with eternal

    _____ at your right hand.

3. Think of a time when all felt right with the world. Where were you? Who were you with? What time of year was it? What were you doing? Include all the details you can remember.

If you have a picture from the time you described, place it where you will see it often this week, and each time you do, thank God for one of the details you listed above.

4. Read **Proverbs 14:30a** and fill in the blanks:

A _____ at _____ gives _____ to the

body ...

A heart at peace: life-giving, refreshing, necessary. The antithesis of stress, worry and fear.

God's word says it's true. Medical science says it's true. So why do we find it so hard to live unrushed and unhurried — to experience the peace of life in the slow lane?

5. Take a **Five-Minute Challenge** this week.

    Each day for the next week, find a quiet place — a favorite chair, lying in bed as you wake or before you fall asleep, at a local park, in your backyard, sitting on your front porch or even at your kitchen table. Turn off the radio, TV and computer screen. Set aside your cell phone. Close your eyes. Take a deep breath. Then listen quietly for five minutes.

    What do you hear?

    -   the hum of the refrigerator
    -   a neighbor's lawnmower
    -   a dog barking
    -   children playing
    -   a train in the distance
    -   the rustle of sheets
    -   leaves dancing in the breeze

    What do you feel?

    -   lonely
    -   frustrated
    -   angry
    -   warm
    -   cold
    -   anxious
    -   calm
    -   pain

    At the end of your five minutes, turn to the **Presence Journal Pages** at the end of this chapter and describe your experience. As you move through the week, see if your experience changes. Do you look forward to the stillness or do you avoid it? Do you feel less rushed, hurried, worried, anxious? Are you beginning to notice more, to be present in the moments of your day?

6. Read **Exodus 33:14** and fill in the blanks:

The Lord replied, "My _____ will go _____ you, and I

will give you _____."

The Israelites had just been told to leave home, to rise up out of Egypt and journey to the Promised Land, flowing with milk and honey, but they'd also been told God would not go with them, for they were a stiff-necked people — stubborn, wanting their own way, wrestling with God for control of their lives. **Exodus 33:4** says, "*When the people heard these distressing words, they began to mourn ...*"

They knew what it meant to live in God's presence *even* through 400 years of slavery. Slavery was awful, but losing God's presence was worse.

By verse 14, Moses was questioning God, asking for reassurance, begging God to teach him, so that he and the people he was leading would continue to find favor with Him.

Our circumstances might be abject, we might not think we can survive for one more day enslaved to illness, but God says, "My Presence will go with you, and I will give you rest."

God promises that He is *with* us. Emmanuel.

GOING DEEPER:

7. Read **Matthew 11:28** and fill in the blanks:

_____ to me, _____ you who are _____

and _____, and I will give you _____.

Today, set aside a few moments to simply *be* in God's presence. No rush. No hurry. No agenda. Just quiet moments in the presence of the One who loves you beyond all measure, *as is*, exactly as you are. The One who invites you to "Come ... and I will give you rest."

8. When do you feel most relaxed, most at peace, most content? Think about a specific time, one that stands out in your memory. What were the circumstances? *Why* did you feel at peace?

9. Now take a few minutes and describe what chronic illness is like for you. Choose a moment or an activity and be as specific as you can.

PRESSING ON:

10. Read **John 15:9b**.

    Now _____ in my _____.

    Read each word slowly. Think about them individually. Read them again. Pause. Allow them to sink in. How do you feel when you read these words? What do they mean to you? What happens to your breathing and heart rate? What happens to the thoughts in your mind? Spend a few minutes journaling your answers to these questions.

    Then when you're ready, turn the page and begin to explore the ancient practice of **Lectio Divina** — *holy reading*.

PRAYER:

Lord, Creator of breath, Creator of time, even as I offer this time to You I realize and accept that the gift is mine. Remind me to still myself in Your presence, to release myself, my cares and my pain to You, even if just for a few minutes each day. Remind me that stillness has purpose, for it is in Your presence that I find myself most whole. Amen.

Presence Journal

Presence Journal

Reading, as it were,
puts food whole into the mouth,
meditation chews it and breakes it up,
prayer extracts its flavor,
contemplation is the sweetness itself,
which gladdens and refreshes.

Guigo II

Lectio Divina

THE PRACTICE OF HOLY READING

Lectio Divina is the ancient practice of slowly, contemplatively reading the words of Scripture, an invitation to encounter God through His Word, to pay close attention, to be fully present.

As we step into the practice of *holy reading*, we begin to discover the underlying spiritual rhythm of our lives, a rhythm sewn into the creation of the world. Day follows night. Tides rise and fall. Months and seasons change as we note the waxing and waning of the moon. And we learn to celebrate new life, sometimes even as we grieve significant loss.

Lectio Divina helps us to reconnect with the eternal rhythm of our lives in five stages:

1. Silence
2. Reading
3. Meditation
4. Prayer
5. Contemplation

The best way to learn a new practice is through experience, so let's begin together with the words of **Isaiah 58:11**.

1. SILENCE

Choose a quiet place, settle into a comfortable position, close your eyes and allow the distractions of the day — all the voices clamoring for your attention — to slide away. Feel your shoulders relax. Notice the rhythmic beating of your heart. Begin to notice the presence of God as you breathe in. As you breathe out, release the burdens, pressures and fears of your day.

2. READING

Lectio is a way of reading patiently and slowly, of listening for God's still, small voice in His Word.

When you're ready, read the words of **Isaiah 58:11**.

Read slowly. Focus on each word. Allow yourself time to simply *be* with God in the words, listening for a word or phrase that captures your heart. Underline, circle or highlight the word or phrase.

> *The Lord will guide you always,*
> *he will satisfy your needs in a sun-scorched land*
> *and will strengthen your frame.*
> *You will be like a well-watered garden,*
> *like a spring whose waters never fail.*

3. MEDITATION

Meditation is our response to God's Word, an invitation to drink in and savor, to allow God to meet us where we are, and to touch us soul-deep.

Explore your thoughts on the **Journal Pages** at the end of this chapter as you answer these questions:

- What does the word or phrase you underlined, circled or highlighted above mean to you in the current circumstances of your life?
- Is there something you might need to change?
- Someone you need to forgive?
- Something you need to release — fear, frustration, control, worry, anger, apathy, anxiety?
- What did you feel when the word or phrase first caught your attention?
- What might God be saying to you through this word or phrase?

4. PRAYER

Prayer is a unique and personal experience, a place of communion and conversation with God. Sometimes we come with words, sometimes we simply come with the groanings of our heart.

It's OK to:
- wrestle with God
- ask, seek or plead with Him
- thank Him
- pause in wonder and awe
- sing
- worship
- weep
- hold God at arm's length
- lean in close without words at all

Sometimes, in a dry season, we can use the words of others to enter into prayer:

You are a fire that takes away the coldness, illuminates the mind with its light, and causes me to know your truth. — Saint Catherine of Siena

Oh, God, give me stillness of soul in You. Rule me, O King of gentleness, King of peace. — Saint John of the Cross

Lord, lead me.

There is no right or wrong way to pray.

Prayer is simply, profoundly, mysteriously, intimately, powerfully how we enter into the presence of God.

5. CONTEMPLATION

This is where we lean into God's embrace and rest in His presence. Contemplation is the stage of surrender — deep, intimate, sometimes tearful, often too deep for words — a quiet rest in the presence of the One who spoke creation into being, who formed man from the dust of the earth and breathed life into him, who formed Eve from Adam's rib, who created *us* in His image.

Lectio Divina is an encounter with God in His Word. As we begin to discover Him in the words of Scripture, we will also begin to see Him more clearly in the world He has created. Lectio helps us to reconnect with the spiritual rhythms of our lives, inviting us to experience the depth of God's love for us, His presence in every moment, every breath and every heartbeat of our lives.

Lectio Divina is an opportunity to slow down and experience God's Word deeply. An opportunity to savor the words of Scripture, to sit at God's table, to be nourished, fed and refreshed. An invitation to be fully present with our holy God.

Lectio Divina Journal

Lectio Divina Journal

Love is a willingness to sacrifice.
Michael Novak

Willingness 3

The evening of our wedding reception, my husband stood and announced to every single human being present that he hoped we'd one day be the parents of six kids. *Six?* Was he serious? Who has six kids these days?

"Wrong wife," I chuckled. I wanted one child, maybe two.

We celebrated our first anniversary with our newborn son in our arms and I knew we'd have more. I'd fallen in love with motherhood. By our fifth anniversary, we had two sons and two daughters, and while I loved our gaggle of children, I also longed for nights of sound sleep, meals without high chairs, no more diapers and time to think in full sentences. I thought our family was complete. My husband graciously agreed, but quietly hoped for more.

Months later, after returning from a business trip, he gathered our kids together and told them all about "this family I met at the airport with five young kids." I watched his face, the longing in his eyes and prayed silently, "God, You know my heart. You know I don't want another child. I'm content and I'm tired. Yet what if that's what You want for us? What if that's Your will for our lives? If somehow it is, You're going to have to change my heart and give me that desire."

I woke the next morning thinking, "I could almost imagine having another baby." And my very next thought was, "God, you are so not funny." That's not the answer I'd expected and not the one I wanted.

But God wasn't the least bit daunted by my attitude, and He didn't diminish this new desire for another child, so I finally told my husband, "I think God wants us to have another baby."

"Really? Are you sure? I won't ask you to go through that again. But," he added with a grin, "I will pray about it."

Nine months later, Megan arrived — a joy, a blessing and *a promise* — for her birth confirmed the beautiful truth of Isaiah 48:17b: "I am the Lord your God, who teaches you what is best for you, who directs you in the way you should go." I'm so grateful God didn't leave me to my own designs. I would have missed so much.

My husband's hope to one day be the father of six was also fulfilled within those nine months, albeit differently than he had dreamed, for Megan was a twin. Her tiny twin was gone almost before we knew she was there, but we both recognized this mysterious, incomprehensible gift. For one day, just beyond the veil, we will meet our precious sixth child.

But Megan's life was also the *promise of hope*, for she was born just six weeks before my brother's sudden death at age 32, leaving behind his toddler son and his wife three months pregnant with their second son.

In the eternal rhythms of creation, we celebrated new life even as we grieved heart-rending loss.

STEPPING IN:

1. Willingness can be a difficult choice, sometimes causing us to feel anxious, frustrated, overwhelmed, angry or afraid. Is there a tension you've been wrestling with? Something you can't quite put your finger on?

2. Read **Jeremiah 29:11** and fill in the blanks:

    "For I know the _____ I have for you," _____ the Lord,

    "plans to _____ you and _____ to _____

    you, plans to give you _____ and a _____."

3. Illness doesn't often *seem* like a plan to prosper and not to harm. It seems like the opposite. Far from helping us find our purpose in life, illness seems to shrink, sap or destroy our purpose. Let's explore this for a bit.

    What was your life's purpose before illness?

Was it tied to your education, occupation, or serving others in your church or community?

What defined you before illness?

4. Read **Micah 6:8** and fill in the blanks:

He has showed you, O man, what is _____. And what does the Lord

_____ of you? To _____ _____and to

_____ _____ and to _____

_____ with your God.

5. How does **Micah 6:8** define purpose?

GOING DEEPER:

6. Look again at both the things that defined you and your life's purpose before illness. How do they align with **Micah 6:8**?

Often culture determines our purpose. We grow up expecting to meet specific social norms, but illness can wedge a wrench in our expectations and in the expectations of those around us.

I often remind my son Sam that every single day he gets out of bed is a *victory*. Every day he rises to greet one more day, even if it's just to sit in his chair, is worth celebrating.

Purpose from God's perspective looks entirely different than purpose from culture's perspective.

7. Where can you shift the paradigm today? Where can you celebrate victory?

8. For the next two days, write down everything that makes your heart sing, everything you love — *anything and everything* — on the **Journal Pages** at the end of this section. We'll use this list a little later in the study, so keep it handy in the coming weeks and continue to list everything that comes to mind.

PRESSING ON:

9. Read **2 Corinthians 8:12** and fill in the blanks:

For if the _____ is there, the _____ is _____ according to what one _____, not according to what he does _____ have.

Spend a little time with this verse — perhaps in **Lectio Divina**. How does it affect your understanding of purpose in chronic illness?

PRAYER:

Lord, in the words of Isaiah 48:17, thank you for who You are, for teaching me what is best for me, and for directing me in the way I should go. In Jesus' holy, precious name, amen.

Willingness Journal

Willingness Journal

Loss cascades across our lives
like autumn leaves

in a chill November wind.
Days, brittle and bleak,

crumble into winter,
till hands arc past midnight

piercing winter-weary souls
with spring.

Cindee Snider Re

Surrender

Late one afternoon, I poured myself a cup of tea, sat my oldest son down and said, "OK, what's going on? You've been cranky and irritable for two days now."

"I'm a spoiled rich kid, Mom. I have too much stuff and I don't appreciate any of it."

Definitely not what I was expecting to hear. "Well, you're right," I said. "According to world standards, you are rich, but you also have a choice."

"Meaning?"

"Your Dad and I struggled with the same thing many years ago. We were bored and discontent, always looking for the next thing to do, the next new thing to buy. We were selfish and self-focused and had a lot of stuff, and it all needed to be stored and cleaned and cared for. We also gave very little."

"So?"

"So we decided to do something radical. We decided to sell and give away a lot of our stuff – almost half of what we owned – because we believed it was the only way we'd learn to be content."

"Was it hard?"

"Most of it was pretty easy, but there were a few things that were very hard. For your dad, it was selling his collection of limited-edition wildlife art prints. For me, it was selling my engagement ring."

"You sold your ring?"

"Yes. And it was hard. It was a very beautiful, very expensive ring, and it had become a huge source of pride for me. I *wanted* people to notice it, to comment on it, to be a little jealous of it. I'm embarrassed to admit that now, but that's exactly *why* I had to let it go. We replaced it with a simple, $60 gold band."

"Did you ever regret it?"

"Honestly, I did. The minute we sold it, I was afraid I'd made a huge mistake, yet as the days passed, a quiet peace settled in.

"I learned I didn't have to be defined by what I have or don't have, what I wear, what I drive, how much we own.

"Kyle, you *do* have a lot, but that also means you also have a choice. Spend some time in prayer. Seek God in this season of discontent, then boldly follow His lead."

"What do you mean?"

"God always has a bigger plan. He always has a purpose for what we experience in life. I had no idea at the time that God had a plan for my ring and our bare walls, but He did. He's filled our home with *your* artwork, Kyle. And just a few months before my brother died, he designed a small, absolutely perfectly understated ring for me — worth infinitely more than all God asked me to surrender all those years ago."

STEPPING IN:

1. Read **Luke 12:15** and fill in the blanks:

    Then He said to them, "_____ _____! Be on your

    _____ against all kinds of _____; a man's life does not

    consist in the _____ of his _____."

2. Life is so much more than our possessions, yet one of the realities of chronic illness is that we sometimes have to give up things we wouldn't *choose* to give up — like a car we can no longer drive, a house we can no longer manage, a favorite pair of shoes we are no longer safe wearing, equipment we once used to play our favorite sport or enjoy our favorite hobby. Sometimes the things we have to give up are less tangible — a job, a vacation, a college education, outings with friends, walking around the block or even walking to the mailbox.

    What is one thing you've had to relinquish because of illness?

3. The apostle Paul was a man familiar with pain and suffering. Three times he asked, begged and pleaded with God to remove the thorn from his side. Three times, God said no. Scholars have long debated exactly what the thorn represents, but one suggestion is physical illness.

    Read Philippians **4:12a** and fill in the blanks:

    I know what it is to be in _____, and I know what it is to

    have _____. I have learned the _____

    of being _____ in any and _____

    situation...

4. Surrender is an incredibly difficult topic in light of chronic illness, because loss is often continued and sustained.

    Take a few minutes this week to think about the losses you've experienced. Begin to list them in the **Journal Pages** at the end of this section.

5. Think about the losses you've been listing, about how you felt when each loss was fresh and new. From the perspective of time, is there a loss you could now describe as *good*? Perhaps not the loss itself, but something good that happened because of it?

    If this is difficult, maybe an example will help. Fourteen years ago, my five kids and I were involved in a serious car accident. My kids' injuries healed in time. Mine did not. For years, I couldn't understand why God would allow me to sustain a permanent injury, sidelining me from serving in ways I loved, ways I was good at. Then my 15-year-old son got sick and never got well. In his hardest moments, in the still of the night, he sought me, because in his words, "You understand. I don't have to explain pain to you. You just get it." He spoke three simple sentences and I understood why my injuries are permanent. Every hard moment, all the pain, each loss, had prepared me to walk beside my son. In a heartbeat, it was worth it. A decade later, it still is.

6. The apostle Paul writes about the "good" in his suffering a little differently. Read **2 Corinthians 12:7** and fill in the blanks.

    To keep me from becoming _____ ... there was given to me a

    _____ in my _____ ...

GOING DEEPER:

7. How do you feel about the passage above? It's OK to wrestle with the idea of finding good in loss. Take some time today to write about this in the **Journal Pages** at the end of this section. No one ever has to read what you write.

    If you have trouble with this, consider writing a letter to God. Sometimes, "Dear God" is all it takes to unlock the words we've tucked deep into the shadowy corners of our souls. Allow the words to spill across the page. Allow the emotion. Be just as kind to yourself as you would be with a friend.

8. Read **John 12:24** and fill in the blanks:

    I tell you the truth, unless a _____ of wheat _____ to

    the ground and _____, it remains only a _____ seed.

    But if it dies, it _____ many _____.

9. Sustained loss can sometimes seem never-ending, like a bleak, eternal winter of the soul. Yet spring *always* returns. Even on the heels of the longest, coldest winter, tender new growth emerges from once frozen soil. Where do you sense the first gentle rays of new growth, the first new seeds from the kernel of loss?

PRESSING ON:

10. Read **Micah 7:7** and fill in the blanks:

    But as for _____, I _____ in _____ for

    the Lord, I _____ for God my Savior; my God will

    _____ _____.

Hope. Precious, tender, promised, spring-fresh hope.

PRAYER:

Gracious God, as I offer this prayer to You, help me to release those things that squeeze out hope and deny Your presence and purpose in my life — possessions, pain, anxiety and impatience. Let me sing in my heart the words of the hymn "I Surrender All." Yes, Lord, "All to Jesus I surrender. Make me, Savior, wholly thine. May Thy Holy Spirit fill me. May I know Thy power divine." With open heart and open hands, Lord, I surrender all. Amen.

Surrender Journal

Surrender Journal

A flower cannot blossom without sunshine,
and man cannot live without love.

Max Müller

Love

"May God break my heart so completely that the whole world falls in," wrote Mother Teresa. Her words have challenged me for years. When I first read them, I thought of world hunger, corrupt governments, AIDS orphans, terrorism and disease. My view has broadened to include my neighbors who are recently divorced, a dear friend who is desperately lonely, the weariness of a mom tenderly caring for her special needs child, the hopelessness of one caught in addiction, the reality of chronic illness.

Sometimes I feel helpless in the midst of all this brokenness.

One afternoon, my neighbor called. She'd recently had surgery and has lived with Parkinson's Disease for several years. She told me her husband, her primary caregiver, needs surgery to remove a malignant brain tumor. My heart broke. I offered meals and help with house and yard work, but it's a short-term solution. They need so much more help than I can provide.

Saturday evening, a friend called, pouring out her heart over a loved one's struggle with addiction. "How do you help someone who doesn't want help?" she asked. Honestly, I don't know. I only know that God is bigger than brain tumors and breast cancer and Parkinson's, bigger than addiction, bigger than any amount of help I can offer.

We want so much to diagnose a problem and offer an immediate solution, but often there are no easy answers, no quick fixes.

And maybe that's just it.

Maybe it's less about what we can *do* than about how much we can *love*. More about walking with others *through* the pain than seeking solutions *for* the pain.

Maybe presence is our greater purpose.

STEPPING IN:

1. What is the most frustrating "solution" someone has offered you?

2. What is the *best* thing someone has done for you?

3. What would be the greatest gift of love you could receive?

4. Think of someone who is struggling, sad, lonely, ill, recovering from surgery or out of a job. What could you do to let them know they're not alone, forgotten or invisible? It doesn't need to be big to be meaningful. It could be a text or a note, a phone call or a visit. You could write a prayer and mail it, or invite them to join you for coffee or lunch. Choose one thing, write it here, and after you've completed it, write your reaction, what it meant to *you* to reach out to another in love.

5. What if purpose looks different than what we often believe? What if purpose is more about presence than occupation or service?

    Read **Galatians 5:6b, 5:14, 6:10** and fill in the blanks:

    5:6b: The _____ thing that counts is _____ expressing

    itself through _____.

    5:14: The _____ law is _____ up in a

    _____ command: "_____ your _____ as

    _____."

    6:10: Therefore, as we have _____, let us do _____ to

    _____ people, especially to those who belong to the

    _____of believers.

6. What have you always believed your purpose to be?

GOING DEEPER:

7. Our purpose in life has less to do with our circumstances, education, job title, relationship status, skills or talents than with God's heart for His people.

    Read **Psalm 36:5-7** and fill in the blanks:

    Your _____, O Lord, reaches to the _____, your

    _____ to the skies. Your righteousness is like the

    _____ mountains, your justice like the _____ deep. O

    Lord, you _____ both man and beast. How _____ is

    your _____ love!

8. Jesus, the Son of God, turned the paradigm of purpose upside down when He walked this earth. He wasn't born into power or the ruling class. He had no wealth, status or noteworthy education. He held no prominent business, legal or political position, and He wasn't recognized for exceptional skill, ability or knowledge. Jesus was born into an ordinary, working-class, Middle Eastern family. Yet His purpose was extraordinary. The same could be said for His disciples. They were ordinary men from ordinary families whose purposes were *extraordinary*.

    If the most extraordinary people in the Bible were ordinary people living ordinary lives, until they were called by God, what does that mean for you?

    Think of Saul, who became Paul. Well educated, well known, well connected, with a career on the fast track, yet none of that fitted him for kingdom work. Instead, he was blinded on the road to Damascus and taken to the very people he'd been hunting to kill.

Think of Moses. Raised as the adopted son of Pharaoh's daughter. Well educated, well known, well connected, with the world at his feet, yet none of it fitted him for God's work. Instead, he killed a man, fled for his life and lived as a shepherd for years in the hill country before God called him.

Our purpose isn't determined by education or wealth or cultural status. It isn't defined by who we know, what we do or where we live. And it isn't affected by what we may have lost because of chronic illness, because our purpose can only come from God.

So what does that mean for you?

What are the things you still *can do* in this hard place? List all that come to mind. Here are a couple of questions to get you started.

Can you pray, text or make a phone call? Write a letter, journal, knit, crochet, quilt, sew, scrapbook, drive, hike, take pictures, make a meal, read to a child? Ask God to show you the things you *can do* in this hard place and list them here.

9. Read **1 Corinthians 10:31** and fill in the blanks:

So   whether   you   _____   or   _____   or

_____ you _____, _____ it all for the

_____ of _____.

PRESSING ON:

10. What does **1 Corinthians 10:31** mean to you in terms of presence? In terms of purpose? Take some time over the next few days to pray through this verse. Ask God to begin to replace culture's definition of purpose with *His* definition of purpose for your life.

PRAYER:

Oh, Lord, sometimes it's easier to love my neighbor than myself, for I am broken in body and spirit. But You can take all that I am and everything I am not, and use it for Your good purpose. We are created to love and be loved by You and one another. Show me how to be Your heart and hands in this world for the people you love so deeply. Amen.

Love Journal

Love Journal

Do not despise the day of small beginnings
Every venture starts with a pang in the heart
Each calling we receive is conceived as a
tiny seed. All holy acts are germinated
arriving like a softly whispered word we
often strain to hear, waiting as it sounds
again, watching as God sends needful food
and rain, nurturing these tiny shoots
now springing fresh from faith-filled roots.
Joy Lenton, Poet

Purpose

Writing a Biblical Purpose Statement
Cindee Snider Re with Pamela K. Piquette

What is purpose?

By definition, purpose encompasses our intentions and objectives. It's the reason something exists or was created, the reason we act or choose not to act.

Often when we think of purpose, we think in terms of employment, relationship status (daughter, son, friend, husband, wife, mother, father, neighbor), volunteer or service work, or contributions to society. And while those are good and valuable, they are only a partial definition.

For it is our biblical purpose that aligns us with God, revealing who we are and why we're here, why we were created.

Understanding our God-given purpose is a process that takes time and a little breathing space, more of an exploration than an exercise — a shedding of our culturally defined purpose to reveal our eternal purpose.

There are no right or wrong answers, no comparisons and no rankings. Purpose is woven into the very fibers of your soul by the One with a plan and a purpose for every single part of His creation.

The following seven verses will help you begin to lay a scriptural foundation for purpose. Offer yourself the gift of unrushed, unhurried time this week to prayerfully work through the verses and answer the questions that follow.

Ecclesiastes 12:13b: Fear God and keep his commandments, for this is the whole duty of man.

1 Corinthians 10:31: So whether you eat or drink or whatever you do, do all to the glory of God.

Psalm 150:6: Let everything that has breath praise the LORD!

Matthew 22:37-39: "You shall love the Lord your God with all your heart and with all your soul, and with all your mind." This is the first and greatest commandment. The second is like it, "Love your neighbor as yourself."

Matthew 5:44-45: But I tell you: Love your enemies and pray for those who persecute you, that you may be sons of your Father in heaven.

1 Thessalonians 5:16-18: Be joyful always; pray continually; give thanks in all circumstances, for this is God's will for you in Christ Jesus.

Micah 6:8: He has showed you, O man, what is good. And what does the LORD require of you? To act justly and to love mercy and to walk humbly with your God.

1. According to **Ecclesiastes 12:13b**, what is the *whole duty of man*?

2. How are these important to understanding your biblical purpose?

3. **1 Corinthians 10:31** asks us to do three things *all to the glory of God*. List them here.

4. Two of those are everyday activities, things we often pay little attention to or take for granted. How do those affect your understanding of purpose?

5. **Psalm 150:6** widens the circle beyond human beings to *everything that has breath*, reminding us that purpose includes what specific activity?

6. How does praise challenge, contradict or reinforce your current understanding of purpose?

7. **Matthew 22:37** calls us to _____ God in three specific ways. List them here.

8. **Matthew 22:39** calls us to _____ our _____ as ourselves.

9. How would embracing these two commandments radically shift your understanding of purpose?

10. If we are truly called to no greater purpose than to love God with all our heart, soul and mind, and to love others as we love ourselves, what happens to our cultural definition of purpose?

11. **Matthew 5:44** again widens the scope and asks us to _____

   our _____ and _____ for those who

   _____ us, further deepening and broadening our

   understanding of purpose, why we're here, why we were created.

12. **1 Thessalonians 5:16-18** calls us to be _____ always,

   _____ continually; and give _____ in all

   circumstances.

   How does that affect purpose, why we were created, why we're here?

13. **Micah 6:8** calls us "To _____ _____ and to

_____ _____ and to _____

_____ with your God."

14. Why might these specific actions (to act justly, love mercy, and walk humbly) be important in defining your purpose?

15. What does it mean to *act justly*? To be just is to be fair. Are you fair in your daily interactions with people?

16. To be merciful is to show compassion or forgiveness to someone who has wronged you. How does *loving mercy* flesh out our biblical purpose?

17. Why do you think God specifically calls us to *love mercy* rather than calling us to act or walk or simply be merciful?

If we look at the specific actions listed in these seven passages, we can begin to build the framework for our own biblical Purpose Statements:

- fear God
- keep His commands
- praise Him
- love Him with all your heart, soul and mind
- love others — neighbors and enemies
- pray continually
- be joyful
- give thanks in all things
- do everything to the glory of God

We live in a culture filled with voices suggesting we can have it all, do it all, be it all.

Discerning God's purpose for our lives with all these external influences can be challenging, yet often less difficult than our own internal struggles with shame, guilt and comparison. When we add the unique challenges of living with chronic illness, prioritizing becomes even more difficult.

Romans 12:2a says, "Do not conform any longer to the pattern of this world, but be transformed by the renewing of your mind."

Let's take a few minutes to throw off old wineskins — those discouraging, bullying, shame-heaping, guilt-laden voices we've lived with for too long.

It might help to identify where we're conforming to the patterns of this world.

1. List anything you feel guilt or shame for *not doing*.

2. List anything you feel guilt or shame *for doing*.

3. Describe a time when you felt at peace. List as many sensory details as you can remember. Where were you? What was happening? What month or season of the year was it? What were you doing? Were you alone or with others? Is there a specific smell, taste or sound you remember?

4. Where does self-care rank as a priority in your life? Not medical care (e.g., doctor appointments, physical therapy, taking medications, etc.), but things like rest, good nutrition, drinking enough water, whatever physical activity is tolerated or medically OK for you to do, etc.

5. Where do reading, writing, hobbies or other enjoyable activities rank as a priority in your life?

You might be thinking, "How can I possibly participate in enjoyable activities when I'm consumed with caring for myself or another with chronic illness?"

We want you to know, you are not alone. At times, we've been so weary it seemed impossible to do *anything* simply for the joy of it. Yet God encourages us to put our hope in Him, "who richly provides us with everything for our enjoyment" (**1 Timothy 6:17b**).

Those words have been hard for me to read some days. Other days, they've made me angry, and sometimes, they've made me cry. But what I've learned over the last 16 years is that it's important to step away, even for just a moment — long enough to close my eyes and breathe, long enough to feel a cup of tea warming my hands, long enough to notice the silvery dust dancing through shadow and light, long enough to be still and remember that He is God. (Cindee)

Today, if you're in that place, start with just 30 seconds. Pause right where you are with this four-word prayer: "Lord, lead the way."

6. List any areas in which you feel guilt or shame that you aren't able to do enough (because of chronic illness or other factors) for the people in your life (family, friends, co-workers, etc.).

7. Think about the ways you currently connect with God — through prayer, reading the Bible, through daily or weekly devotionals or Bible studies, in nature, through music, by journaling, etc. — and list them here.

NOW, LET'S START OVER

Your Purpose Statement can be a bullet list of priorities or a single, more formal sentence. Ideally, it will be short and easy to remember, a unique description of who you are in Christ.

We all share the same goal — to love and follow Jesus — yet the way we each do that will look a little bit different.

STEP ONE

Take some time today to think beyond illness and its impact on your life — a little room to dream, something you may not have done for many months or for even many years. Give yourself permission to remember and also to hope, and when you're ready, begin to journal your answers to the following questions.

1. List all the things you care about.

2. List the things you love, your passions, things that make your heart sing.

3. What are you most interested in (e.g.: sports, history, gardening, crafts, the arts, literature, music, movies, travel, education, hobbies, etc.)?

4. List words and phrases that positively describe you (e.g.: teacher, gardener, reader, listener, encourager, visionary, compassionate, kind, understanding, generous, wise, discerning, etc.).

5. In what ways have you enjoyed serving, now or in the past?

7. What dream, hope, vision or mission has God planted in your heart? Don't edit or limit your dream because you think it's impossible. Write boldly, courageously whatever God has placed on your heart.

I once told my husband, "Dreams weren't meant for someone like me." I was in a dark place and had been for several years. Friends of mine were publishing books and speaking, hosting retreats and conferences, and I honestly believed it was safer to give up on my dream than continue to cradle hope's fading embers. But I was wrong. God had placed a dream in my heart. He had a plan and a purpose — far greater than I ever dared to imagine. Deep breath, Warriors! In faith, courageously write your dream. (Cindee)

Remember that your Purpose Statement will likely transform as you continue to grow in Christ and your understanding of His purpose for your life. This isn't meant to be a static statement, but a starting point, a place to dip your oar in the current of God's greater plan for your life.

STEP TWO

1. Now reread your answers in STEP ONE. Circle or highlight the most important word or phrase to you in each question and list those word or phrases here.

2. Begin to work with your list. Prioritize, categorize, combine or group your ideas. Play with the words and phrases and begin to structure them into bullet points or sentences.

3. Over the next few weeks, work toward a simple list of bullet points or a single sentence and write it here.

4. Let's look again at the biblical framework for purpose:
   - fear God
   - keep His commands
   - praise Him
   - love Him with all your heart, soul and mind
   - love others — neighbors and enemies
   - pray continually
   - be joyful
   - give thanks
   - do everything to the glory of God

5. Is your Purpose Statement beginning to reflect who you are in Christ? Who He created you to be?

6. When your Purpose Statement is complete, write it here.

Consider writing your Purpose Statement on a notecard and taping it to your bathroom mirror or writing it on an index card and tucking it in the front cover of your Bible. If you're crafty, print it on a bookmark or place it in a frame and display it where you will see it often.

Now that you've written your Purpose Statement, we thought you'd enjoy reading the statements of some of the people close to Chronic Joy Ministry.

I was created to hold hope, seek beauty, chase light and dance with words, because that is how I experience the presence of God and speak life to a broken, hurting world.

CINDEE SNIDER RE
Author and Co-Founder of Chronic Joy Ministry, Inc.

I believe that I was created to impact the world in unique ways that build community and serve others. To do so, I must take good care of me spiritually, physically, emotionally and mentally.

- *Spiritually: staying connected to my Heavenly Father through prayer and Scripture, and to a local body of believers*
- *Physically: following, to the best of my ability, the treatment plans my medical team and I have developed*
- *Emotionally: accepting that my limitations are not punishments, but a necessary part of the unique work God has given me to do. A nap or rest, for example, provides the necessary fuel to accomplish His plan. Perhaps it allows me to simply hear His still small voice for I am still.*
- *Mentally: seeking therapy or support when needed to guide me through the challenges that living with chronic illness brings.*

PAMELA PIQUETTE
President and Co-Founder of Chronic Joy Ministry, Inc.

Ground myself in God's understanding, such that unconditional love flows through me.

RACHEL THIEL
Physical Therapist and Chronic Joy Ministry, Inc. Board Member

I am redeemed and strengthened by His grace — daily seeking to grow ever deeper in His love and called to share His hope, always.

GINA M. WEEKS
Feedback Teams for *Discovering Hope* and *Finding Purpose*

To love God with my whole heart, soul and mind. To love myself and others as God loves us all.

HEATHER MACLAREN JOHNSON
Clinical Psychologist and Chronic Joy Ministry, Inc. Board Member

At Jesus' birth, the three Kings presented Him with gifts that revealed His purpose. At our birth, the King of kings and the whole realm of the Trinity bestowed on us gifts that define our purpose. Some gifts are evident. Others await discovery. All are filled with promise. As I seek the will of the Giver and use my gifts for His Glory, He will reveal my full potential.

This is my prayer. This is my purpose. This is The Point.

(The Point - A Garden Message is the title of my book, the name God revealed to me and confirmed while I was working in the gardens of Zion Episcopal Church.)

MARY ELIZABETH CASEY
Feedback Teams for *Discovering Hope* and *Finding Purpose*

Purpose Journal

Purpose Journal

For we are so preciously loved by God
that we cannot even comprehend it.

Julian of Norwich

Refining

"What if God healed you tomorrow?" my daughter asked me one morning. "Would you want to be healed?"

"Hmmm…" I answered, thinking for a few moments. "No," I finally replied, "I don't think I would."

Twelve years ago, in one brief April moment of skidding tires, shrieking metal, breaking glass and inflated airbags, a green Toyota minivan t-boned ours at 50 mph and forever changed our lives.

My kids' injuries healed in time. Mine did not. For three years, I journeyed through tests, procedures, surgeries, medications, specialists, occupational and physical therapy. I hoped for, prayed for and begged for healing, and God said, "No."

"Why wouldn't you want to be healed?" my daughter asked, surprised.

"Well, it's not that I like living with the pain and limitations of my injury, but I'm not sure I'd stay this close to God without them. What if He healed me and I slid back into old habits — hurried, impatient and stressed with no time for people, no time for God, no time to stop and appreciate His incredible creation? Honestly, that would be worse in every way than this."

"But how do you know it wouldn't be different now?"

"I don't know that for sure, but when the pain is less, I still feel the pull to do more, to be more. For the past twelve years, God has proven He's sufficient, more than enough, yet somehow on the better days, I still fight Him for control.

"Maybe God is choosing not to heal me, because He knows my injury is better not only for me, but also for those around me. I might not *like* the pain, but I do like the person I'm becoming because of it."

STEPPING IN:

1. Healing can be a very difficult topic for those of us living with chronic physical and mental illness. Often we've sought more medical care and tried more medications and treatments than we can remember. We've prayed for healing; we've been prayed over; we've cried out to God, pleaded with Him, maybe even bargained with Him; and finally, we've grieved the loss. Yet grieving isn't a one-time event with chronic illness. It's something we experience again and again on this journey.

   Healing can come, but sometimes healing waits for us on the other side of the veil. Yet while we wait, God is *with us* in the suffering, in the pain, in the anxiety and depression, and in our longing to be healed.

   What, for you, is the most difficult aspect of the topic of healing?

2. Describe the best thing you've experienced related to healing.

3. Describe what it might be like to be healed today.

4. Read **2 Corinthians 1:5** and fill in the blanks:

    For just as the _____ of Christ _____ over into

    our _____, so also _____ Christ our

    _____ overflows.

5. Often when we seek comfort, what we long for is healing. If God removed the pain, frustration, discomfort or illness each time we sought His comfort, would we be drawn to Him out of love or simply opportunity?

    Research shows that those who share painful experiences often forge strong bonds with one another. Could illness and pain hold greater purpose than we imagine?

6. Read **Romans 12:15** and fill in the blanks:

    _____ with those who _____; _____

    with those who _____.

    What if pain draws us closer not only to God but also to one another?

GOING DEEPER:

7. Take a few minutes this week to describe an experience of shared pain/hardship/tragedy that forged an unexpected bond with another person.

    Sometimes these are the stories told and retold among family and friends; sometimes they are stories rarely spoken aloud (such as those shared in war). Sometimes the stories can be difficult, yet from the perspective of time, they can also hold an element of humor. Sometimes they are stories illuminating the best of humanity experienced at the scene of an accident or other emergency, or in the aftermath of a natural disaster or national emergency.

    Begin to write your stories of shared experience in the **Journal Pages** at the end of this section.

8. Read **1 Peter 4:12-13** and fill in the blanks:

Dear _____, do not be _____ at the

_____ trial you are _____, as though something

_____ were happening to you. But _____ that

you _____ in the _____ of Christ, so that you may

be _____ when his _____ is revealed.

9. If trials are not strange, but common to all people, how does that begin to change your understanding of purpose in a life with chronic illness?

PRESSING ON:

10. Read **1 Peter 4:19** and fill in the blanks:

So then, those who _____ according to _____ will

should _____ themselves to their _____ Creator

and _____ to do _____ .

We are called by this verse to do two things. What are they?

    1.

    2.

How does committing yourself to God and continuing to do good affect your understanding of purpose right where you are today?

PRAYER:

Gracious Creator, I come to you with hope and prayer for healing, for I do not want this pain in my body, mind or soul to continue. Yet at times, Your answer seems to be no or not yet. Open my heart to see where You are already present and active in my life, healing me in ways I do not always understand. Help me to embrace that in everything, You are with me, loving me and molding me, and giving purpose to all aspects of my life in You. Amen.

Refining Journal

Refining Journal

God wants you to live for others
and to live that presence well.

Henri Nouwen

Attitude

"Did anything surprise you?" my husband asked.

"Not really," I answered a little too quickly. "I could have told you where I'd end up without answering all those questions."

My husband wisely waits me out sometimes.

"Well, I guess one thing surprised me. For the past 24 years, I've been immersed in the area of my greatest weakness. Do you know I scored a zero in the Motivator category? Yet that's what I'm called to do every single day — to motivate, encourage, cheerlead, hold hope, seek beauty, and find of every shred of good in all this hard for those who dwell within these walls. I scored a zero — *nothing, nada, zilch* — in the one thing I'm called to do *every single blessed day*."

The irony wasn't lost on me.

For almost 25 years, God has been chiseling away at my stubborn independence, sanding off my *I-don't-really-like-other-people* edges, teaching me to make eye contact when I'd rather walk right on by, encouraging me to step outside myself where I can be far too content, and placing me in a house spilling over with people — seven who live here full-time and a half dozen more who walk these doors on a regular basis.

God calls me daily to bring my lack, my brokenness, my zero, in exchange for His enough, His strength, His all.

STEPPING IN:

1. Often our desired, planned-for, hoped-for purpose in life is vastly different from God's purpose for our life. When we ask young children what they want to be when they grow up, they enthusiastically respond with things like astronaut, firefighter, garbage collector, doctor, nurse, princess or superhero. Yet how often do those excited five-year-old answers become 35-year-old realities?

   Just for fun, what did you most want to be when you grew up?

2. Culturally, we tend to equate vocation with purpose, and while a career can be part of our eternal purpose, often, especially in a life with chronic illness, it is not. What is it that God calls us to do with these days that we've been given?

   The answer can be found in part in Psalm **46:10a**:

   _____ _____ and _____ that I am

   _____...

3. How does that verse change the way you understand purpose?

4. Now let's look at **Exodus 25:1-2, 8**:

   Vs 1-2: The Lord said to Moses, "Tell the Israelites to bring me an

   _____. You are to receive the offering for _____

   from each man whose _____ prompts him to

   _____....

   Vs 8: "Then have them make a _____ for me, and I will

   _____ among them."

5. The Israelites were called to bring their best gifts: "gold, silver and bronze; blue, purple and scarlet yarn and fine linen; goat hair; ram skins dyed red and hides of sea cows; acacia wood; olive oil for the light; spices for the anointing oil and for the fragrant incense; and onyx stones and other gems." **(Exodus 25:3-7)**

Today, *we* are God's sanctuary, the dwelling place of His Spirit. What can you offer God from your heart today?

6. When you think about God's purpose for this season of your life — where you're living, what you do each day, the people you come into contact with on a regular basis (family, friends, neighbors, doctors, therapists, pharmacist, mail carrier, etc.) — what do you feel? Mark all that apply.

○ frustrated	○ envious/Jealous
○ sad	○ indifferent
○ angry	○ challenged
○ hopeful	○ fearful
○ worthless	○ anxious
○ helpless	○ excited
○ blessed	○ embarrassed
○ bitter	○ guilty/shamed
○ resentful	○ optimistic

GOING DEEPER:

7. Has God called you to an area of weakness, an area you feel ill equipped to function within, somewhere outside of your natural gifts, talents and tendencies?

8. What might God be teaching you in this place?

9. Read **Psalm 100** and fill in the blanks:

Shout for _____ to the Lord, all the earth. _____

the Lord with _____; come before him with

_____ songs. _____ that the Lord is

_____. It is he who _____ us, and we are

_____; we are his _____, the sheep of his pasture.

_____ his gates with _____ and his

_____ with _____; give _____ to

him and _____ his name. For the Lord is _____

and his love _____ forever; his _____ continues

through _____ generations.

PRESSING ON:

10. In **Psalm 100**, we are called to:
    - shout
    - worship
    - sing
    - enter
    - praise
    - give thanks

    This is holy purpose. *This* is what matters for eternity.

    Spend some time this week with the following verses, steeping yourself in God's purpose for your life. There are **Journal Pages** included for your thoughts.

Micah 6:8
He has shown you, O man, what is good,
And what does the Lord require of you?
To act justly and to love mercy
and to walk humbly with your God.

Matthew 22:37
Love the Lord your God with all your heart and with all your soul and with all your mind.

Matthew 22:39b
"Love your neighbor as yourself."

Ecclesiastes 12:13b
Fear God and keep his commandments, for this is the whole duty of man.

Psalm 150:6
Let everything that has breath praise the LORD!

PRAYER:

Lord, show me again and again what is good, for my expectation and understanding are often too small. Teach me to praise You in all things. When I am too weak to shout or sing, let the whispered praise of my heart be strong. And when I am unsure, wondering if what I give is good enough, remind me that Your grace is sufficient. Let me walk humbly with You each day, for that is where joy and purpose abound. Amen.

Attitude Journal

Attitude Journal

*Christianity, while acknowledging
the presence of suffering,
declares that life can be
infinitely worth living...*
Kenneth Scott Latourette

Contentment

I attended a medical conference recently and two things struck me. The first was a refreshing openness and a willing vulnerability among the participants to listen, connect and enter into one another's lives — less about impressing each other with where we live, what we do, or the degrees we hold than about how we are doing, less a casual "How are you?" than a genuine "How are you, *really?*"

The second was perspective. This conference drew patients, caregivers and internationally renowned medical specialists and researchers together for three days of education, updates and the opportunity to meet and connect with one another. While there are currently no cures and few effective treatments for the rare diseases that affect these participants' lives, there is hope, because today, we are alive.

We may be in pain, we may have little energy, we may be struggling with nausea and migraine, but today, we are alive and as long as we draw breath, there is hope.

Because hope is the wellspring of joy, the foundation of contentment.

Pastor Max Ramsey wrote, "It is human to slip into seasons of resentment and ingratitude. It is human to lose perspective when we face trouble, to cling to a grievance and forget the hundreds of blessings. It is human to get so caught up in our own stuff that we forget that others have stuff too. And in those seasons, our joy is lost. But joy is a river over-flowing. And the river of joy can carry us across the river of life. We are all mortal, yet because death is imminent, I remember that you matter, that this moment matters."

Remembering that this world is not all there is, that there *is* something greater waiting in the wings, offers perspective.

That doesn't mean it's easy. That doesn't mean there isn't struggle or pain or tears. But it does mean that whether or not our circumstances change, there *is* hope — the promise of joy and the peace of contentment.

STEPPING IN:

1. Worry is the opposite of contentment and can easily consume us. Luke asks

    a great question in **Luke 12:25**:

    But who of you by _____ can add a single _____

    to his _____ ?

    Let that sink in for a minute.

    Worry is a knock-off bauble masquerading as Truth, but costing us dearly.

2. **Proverbs 12:25a** adds this:

    An _____ heart _____ a man down.

    That knock-off bauble not only costs us our hope, joy, peace and
    contentment, but it also shackles our hearts to fear.

3. Christ offers a better way. You'll find it in **Matthew 6:34a**:

    Therefore _____ _____ _____

    about tomorrow, for tomorrow will _____ about itself.

    Medical science confirms that worry affects appetite, habits, relationships,
    sleep and even our ability to concentrate and retain information. No wonder
    God longs to protect us from that.

4. What are the things you worry about most often?

5. Take some time today to explore what might happen if you offer yourself the freedom to lay your worries at Jesus' feet Imagine unshackling each fear and watching it fall to the ground at the foot of the cross. Use the **Journal Pages** at the end of this chapter to explore these thoughts.

6. When you're ready, turn to **Matthew 11:28-30** and fill in the blanks:

   Come to me, all you who are _____ and _____,

   and I will give you _____. Take my yoke upon you and

   _____ from me, for I am _____ and

   _____ in heart, and you will find _____ for your

   souls. For my yoke is _____ and my burden is

   _____.

GOING DEEPER:

7. Now that you've tasted freedom from worry, let's look at God's promises for His weary children.

   Read the following verses and fill in the blanks:

   Jeremiah 31:25:

   I will _____ the weary and _____ the faint.

   Psalm 104:13b

   … the earth is _____ by the _____

   of his _____ .

   Psalm 145:16

   You open your hand and _____ the _____ of

   _____ _____ thing.

   Isaiah 58:11

   The Lord will _____ you _____; he will

   _____ your needs in a _____-

   _____ land and will _____ your frame. You will be

   like a _____-_____ garden, like a spring whose

   waters never _____ .

8. Turn to the **Journal Pages** where you wrote about worry (Question 5) and reread your words. How do God's promises in **Matthew 11:28-30**, **Jeremiah 31:25**, **Psalm 104:13b**, **Psalm 145:16** and **Isaiah 58:11** (Questions 6 and 7) shift your thinking?

In the space below or on the **Journal Pages**, write a prayer to God releasing your worries and embracing His promises, and include today's date.

9. Now let's switch gears and explore the distinction between worry and concern by writing a short allegory. There are **Allegory Journal Pages** for you to use at the end of this chapter.

    Begin by describing the two main characters — *Worry* and *Concern*. Choose one of the worries you identified in Question 5 and turn it into a "problem" for each of your characters to face.

    How will *Worry* interact with the problem? How about *Concern*? What is the outcome for each?

    Worry will see the problem and be immobilized by it. *Concern* will notice the same problem, but she will pause and begin to gather facts.

    Worry's attention will be focused on the problem, while *Concern's* will be focused on God.

    Which of your characters reacts more like you do? Does that surprise you?

Understanding how we view circumstances can begin to change the way we react to them. Story, because it is relatable, memorable and often unobtrusive, can help us to see through new eyes. Jesus used an ancient form of story, parables, to teach important truths.

Keep your allegory characters in mind this week. Think about how they might react to the various situations you experience. Journal your insights.

PRAYER:

Oh, Lord, another song springs to heart, a song of resurrected life and hope. "Because He lives, I can face tomorrow. Because He lives all fear is gone … And life is worth the living, just because He lives." Let me not be held captive by debilitating worry, but strengthen me to share my joys and concerns with You, free to act in Your will and to rest in your refreshing Spirit. Amen.

Contentment Journal

Contentment Journal

Allegory Journal

Allegory Journal

A single sunbeam is enough to
drive away many shadows.
Saint Francis of Assisi

Choice

Faith is a journey — a choice every minute of every day. I can either choose God or I can choose me. I can choose to seek Him in the midst of the chaos or I can allow my circumstances to overwhelm me. I can choose to live in the power of His Spirit or I can choose to rely on my own strength.

But I can't have it both ways. It's either God or me.

Last week, I chose me. I reacted to a situation with anger. I spoke out of turn and poured fuel on an already burning fire. I didn't pause or think or pray, and I reaped the just rewards, little love and lots of damage.

Yesterday, I woke to a sick son and barking puppies, and I had another choice. I could choose to react or I could choose to be intentionally grateful.

I could choose to focus on the insistent, noisy barking or I could choose to be thankful for the pups' exuberance. I could choose to be overwhelmed that my son was sick or I could choose to be grateful that he was waking in his own bed instead of in his all-too-familiar room at Children's Hospital.

Yesterday, I chose God and it made all the difference, lots of love and little stress.

Why would I ever *willingly* choose me?

STEPPING IN:

1. What happens when we put God first?

   Read Psalm **29:11** and fill in the blanks.

   The Lord gives _____ to his people; the Lord _____ his people with _____.

2. **Isaiah 54:10** adds to the promise.

   "Though the mountains be _____ and the hills be _____, yet my _____ love for you will not be shaken nor my covenant of _____ be removed," says the Lord, who has _____ on you.

   God's love for us is unfailing and His peace is secure, regardless of our circumstances.

3. **Job 12:10** expands our understanding of God's compassion.

   In his hand is the _____ of every _____ and the _____ of all _____.

4. **1 John 4:19** explains why choosing God and putting Him first matters.

   We _____ because he _____ loved us.

   We are able to love only because God *first* loves us. It is God's love flowing *through* us that touches others.

5. **Ephesians 4:2** this is where eternal purpose shines through.

   Be   completely   _____   and   _____ ;   be

   _____ ,   bearing   _____   one   another   in

   _____ .

6. Love is a choice — the ultimate choice. But love isn't easy. Spend some time today listing the ways it's sometimes hard to love those around you — family, friends, medical personnel, cashiers, those who mean well but offer unhelpful advice, etc.

GOING DEEPER:

7. Love, especially when it's hard, is the marrow of faith and purpose. Read **Luke 6:27** and fill in the blanks:

    Love your _____, do _____ to those who

    _____ you, _____ those who _____

    you, _____ for those who _____ you.

8. Look back at your list in Question 6. Let's spin that list 180°. **Luke 6:27** tells us to do four specific things: love, do good, bless and pray. Take some time to look at what you wrote in Question 6, then move each *hard way to love* into one of the four categories below.

    For example: Some days it's hard for me to be patient with those who process my words slowly. Yet if I pause and reflect on Luke 6:27, I'm sometimes able to love, bless or pray for the other person instead of feeling impatience or frustration.

    LOVE   **DO GOOD**   **BLESS**   **PRAY**

9. Now it's time to step into your eternal purpose. Use the lists in Question 8 as a starting point. Each day, choose one *hard way to love* and ask God to show you how to *love* your enemies, *do good* to those who dislike you, *bless* those who speak poorly about you, and *pray* for those who mistreat you.

    There are **Journal Pages** included for you to record each *hard way to love* and how you chose to pour out the precious gift of God's unfailing love.

    Your hard situations may not change, but God will work a beautiful change in you.

10. **Luke 6:38** poignantly illustrates this change.

    _____, and it will be given to _____. A

    _____ measure, _____ down, _____

    together and _____ over, will be _____ into your

    lap.

    You were created for a reason and you are gifted with eternal purpose — to love God and to love others, even when it's hard, maybe especially when it's hard.

    And now it's time. Time to step into *your* eternal purpose.

PRAYER:

Holy and loving God, sometimes I wonder if I make it hard for You to love me, then I hear the truth in my heart — You chose me. Your love is unending and without fail even when I turn away. Teach me to choose to love in pain or in peace, in joy or in sorrow, in healing or in brokenness, for that is the wellspring of purpose. Amen.

Choice Journal

Choice Journal

Whether you understand it or not,
God loves you, is present in you,
lives in you, dwells in you,
calls you, saves you and offers you
an understanding and compassion
which are like nothing
you have ever found in a book
or heard in a sermon.

Thomas Merton

Appendix

Small Group Policy

AS A GROUP, WE WILL:

- Create a space where people feel cared for, prayed for, encouraged and respected — a place people can't wait to return to!
- Limit the group size to six people or fewer to allow each person the opportunity to participate without feeling rushed.
- Recognize that there will be ups and downs and that pain and illness will sometimes cause us to speak or respond in uncharacteristic ways.
- Start and end on time, respecting the energy limits of each member.
- Be open and authentic, creating the opportunity for deeper relationships with each other and with God.
- Engage in discussion, allowing each member a chance to speak and be heard.
- Affirm and respond when someone shares. Vulnerability is risky. Encourage one another.
- Keep what is said here private and confidential.
- Be gracious and kind. We're each affected differently by illness, we're each at a different point in the journey and we may not share the same views on healing, medications, diets, treatments or doctors.
- Let the facilitator know if you won't be there and how the group can pray for you.
- Be considerate of the needs of others by:
    - not wearing perfume, cologne or scented lotions.
    - not soliciting the sale of products or services.
    - offering group members the freedom to sit, stand and move to increase comfort.

SIGN: _____

DATE: _____

Small Group Contact Information

Name:
Address:
Email:
Phone:

Name:
Address:
Email:
Phone:

Name:
Address:
Email:
Phone:

Name:
Address:
Email:
Phone:

Name:
Address:
Email:
Phone:

Name:
Address:
Email:
Phone:

Build an Illness Ministry

STEPPING IN:

WHY DO WE NEED A CHRONIC ILLNESS MINISTRY?

1. Approximately *1 in 2 people* live with one or more chronic illnesses.
2. Mental illness affects *1 in 5 adults*.
3. Many with chronic illness are hurting, lonely and exhausted.
4. Many struggle with anxiety, depression, pain and/or significant limitations.
5. Many with chronic illness don't look sick, so they become an invisible statistic.
6. Chronic illness can be a staggering financial burden. According to the CDC, 86% of all health care spending in 2010 was for people with chronic medical conditions.
7. Chronic illness affects marriage, family, faith, finances, friendships, education, hobbies and work, in short, every aspect of life.

WHAT CAN YOU DO?

1. Start the conversation. Begin with one person you know who has chronic illness. Ask them what it's like. Listen. Try to hear what they might not be saying.
2. Invite a small group to brainstorm about what a chronic illness ministry might look like in your church, neighborhood, work place or organization. Might it include awareness? Resources? Education? A small group? Counseling? Transportation? Meals? Financial assistance?

3. Think about possible service projects. How could this ministry offer opportunities for participants to *invest in others*?
4. Could you offer a Bible study? How often? How long?
5. Think about caregivers. What could you do to help them?

GOING DEEPER:

ONCE YOU'VE DECIDED TO START A MINISTRY

1. *Create a Mission Statement*
   Example: To provide a safe, caring, loving environment in which people can grieve, accept and learn to thrive in a life with chronic illness.

2. *Develop a Vision Statement*
   Example: To facilitate participation between those living with chronic illness and [your organization] – an opportunity to serve and minister to those with chronic illness, including them as vital, necessary and important members, and offering them creative opportunities to serve and be involved.

3. *Small Groups*
   - Consider these four core group values as you launch your first small group: *Hope, Purpose, Worth, Joy* and how these values connect us deeply to God and to one another, how they help us connect, grow and serve right where we are.
   - We suggest bi-weekly meetings of 90 minutes or less.
   - Small groups of up to six participants each are recommended to allow each person the opportunity to share and be heard.
   - Consider the needs of your participants. Will they need:
     - access to bathrooms
     - space for those who may need to occasionally move (e.g.: sit, stand, walk a bit) to be comfortable
     - perhaps a few high tables for those who may need to stand
     - wheelchair accessibility
     - time of day and day of week

- o food restrictions if you offer refreshments
- o cost to participants
- Consider starting a virtual group using Facebook video, Skype or Google Hangouts.

4. *Caregivers*
Caregivers need care too. Consider hosting a group specifically for them.

5. *Resources*
What will you need to facilitate this ministry?
- A place to meet
- Printed materials?
- Curricula?
- Financial support?
- The support of a pastor or trained counselor?
- Email, website, database and/or social media support?
- Refreshments?

6. *Curricula*
- The Chronic Joy Thrive Series – Discovering Hope, Finding Purpose, Embracing Worth and Encountering Joy are specifically designed for chronic illness small groups.

7. *Leaders*
- Who will lead small groups and for how long?
- Will you provide training for them?
- A wealth of resources to equip small group leaders are available at **www.chronic-joy.org**.

PRESSING ON:

8. *Service Opportunities*
How can those in your chronic illness small groups begin to serve others in your church, organization, community or around the world? Here's a short list to get you thinking

- Write cards or letters for those who are hospitalized or homebound.
- Write to soldiers or missionaries serving overseas.

- Make colorful cards for children's meal trays at your local children's hospital.
- Read to a child or for the visually impaired.
- Knit or crochet prayer shawls, baby blankets, mittens, hats or scarves for those who are grieving, facing surgery or in homeless shelters.
- Bake cookies for a youth event, bake sale or for someone who is homebound.
- Send birthday cards to nursing home residents.
- Make "care kits" with shampoo, soap, toothbrushes, deodorant, healthy snacks, etc. to donate to the homeless/homeless shelters.
- Make hospital care bags for those in the hospital or their caregivers – healthy snacks, fruit, homemade cookies or breads, a soft blanket, toothpaste, lotion, a book, puzzle or game, gift cards for gas, the hospital cafeteria, toiletries, etc.
- Create "Birthday in a Bag" kits for local children's shelters. Include party hats, plates, cups, napkins, forks, a cake mix, frosting, candles, etc.

Be creative. Look for opportunities. Brainstorm ideas. Serving unlocks the door to hope.

Reproducible Prayer Card

◐ Prayer

"For where two or three are gathered together in my name, there am I in the midst of them." Matthew 18:20

How you can pray for me this week:

_____

_____

Where I experienced hope this week:

_____

_____

NIV Scripture Used in the Study

CHAPTER 1

Question 2: **Psalm 16:11**
You make known to me the path of life; you will fill me with joy in your presence, with eternal pleasures at your right hand.

Question 4: **Proverbs 14:30a**
A heart at peace gives life to the body ...

Question 6: **Exodus 33:14**
"My Presence will go with you, and I will give you rest."

Question 7: **Matthew 11:28**
Come to me, all you who are weary and burdened, and I will give you rest.

Question 10: **John 15:9b**
Now remain in my love.

CHAPTER 2

Page 12 **Isaiah 58:11**
The Lord will guide you always, He will satisfy your needs in a sun-scorched land and will strengthen your frame. You will be like a well-watered garden, like a spring whose waters never fail.

CHAPTER 3

Question 2: **Jeremiah 29:11**
"For I know the plans I have for you," declares the Lord, "plans to prosper you and not to harm you, plans to give you hope and a future."

Question 5:   **Micah 6:8**
He has showed you, O man, what is good. And what does the Lord require of you? To act justly and to love mercy and to walk humbly with your God.

Question 10:   **2 Corinthians 8:12**
For if the willingness is there, the gift is acceptable according to what one has, not according to what he does not have.

CHAPTER 4

Question 1:   **Luke 12:15**
Then He said to them, "Watch out! Be on your guard against all kinds of greed; a man's life does not consist in the abundance of his possessions."

Question 3:   **Philippians 4:12a**

I know what it is to be in need, and I know what it is to have plenty. I have learned the secret of being content in any and every situation.

Question 6:   **2 Corinthians 12:7**
To keep me from becoming conceited...there was given to me a thorn in my flesh...

Question 8:   **John 12:24**
I tell you the truth, unless a kernel of wheat falls to the ground and dies, it remains only a single seed. But if it dies, it produces many seeds.

Question 10:   **Micah 7:7**
But as for me, I watch in hope for the Lord, I wait for God my Savior; my God will hear me.

CHAPTER 5

Question 5:   **Galatians 5:6b**
The only thing that counts is faith expressing itself through love.

Galatians 5:14
The entire law is summed up in a single command: "Love your neighbor as yourself."

Galatians 6:10
Therefore, as we have opportunity, let us do good to all people, especially to those who belong to the family of believers.

Question 7:   **Psalm 36:5-7**
Your love, O Lord, reaches to the heavens, your faithfulness to the skies. Your righteousness is like the mighty mountains, your justice like the great deep. O Lord, you preserve both man and beast. How priceless is your unfailing love!

Question 9:   **1 Corinthians 10:31**
So whether you eat or drink or whatever you do, do it all for the glory of God.

CHAPTER 6

Ecclesiastes 12:13b
Fear God and keep his commandments, for this is the whole duty of man.

1 Corinthians 10:31
So, whether you eat or drink, or whatever you do, do all to the glory of God.

Psalm 150:6
Let everything that has breath praise the LORD!

Matthew 22:37-39
Jesus replied: "'Love the Lord your God with all your heart and with all your soul, and with all your mind.' This is the first and greatest commandment. And the second is like it: 'Love your neighbor as yourself.'"

Micah 6:8
He has shown you, O man, what is good. And what does the LORD require of you? To act justly and to love mercy and to walk humbly with your God.

1 Timothy 6:17b
...but to put their hope in God, who richly provides us with everything for our enjoyment.

Matthew 5:44
But I tell you: Love your enemies and pray for those who persecute you.

1 Thessalonians 5:16-18
Be joyful always; pray continually; give thanks in all circumstances, for this is God's will for you in Christ Jesus.

CHAPTER 7

Question 4: **2 Corinthians 1:5**
For just as the sufferings of Christ flow over into our lives, so also through Christ our comfort overflows.

Question 6: **Romans 12:15**
Rejoice with those who rejoice; mourn with those who mourn.

Question 8:   **1 Peter 4:12-13**

Dear friends, do not be surprised at the painful trial you are suffering, as though something strange were happening to you. But rejoice that you participate in the sufferings of Christ, so that you may be overjoyed when his glory is revealed.

Question 10:   **1 Peter 4:19**

So then, those who suffer according to God's will should commit themselves to their faithful Creator and continue to do good.

CHAPTER 8

Question 2:   **Psalm 46:10a**

Be still, and know that I am God....

Question 4:   **Exodus 25:1-2**

The Lord said to Moses, "Tell the Israelites to bring me an offering. You are to receive the offering for me from each man whose heart prompts him to give."

Exodus 25:8

"Then have them make a sanctuary for me, and I will dwell among them."

Question 9:   **Psalm 100**

Shout for joy to the Lord, all the earth,
Worship the Lord with gladness;
come before him with joyful songs.
Know that the Lord is God.
It is he who made us, and we are his;
we are his people, the sheep of his pasture.
Enter his gates with thanksgiving
and his courts with praise;
give thanks to him and praise his name.
For the Lord is good and his love endures forever;
his faithfulness continues through all generations.

Question 10:   **Micah 6:8**
He has shown you, O man, what is good, And what does the Lord require of you? To act justly and to love mercy and to walk humbly with your God.

Matthew 22:37
Love the Lord your God with all your heart and with all your soul and with all your mind

Matthew 22:39b
'Love your neighbor as yourself.'

Ecclesiastes 12:13b
Fear God and keep his commandments, for this is the whole duty of man

Psalm 150:6
Let everything that has breath praise the LORD!

CHAPTER 9

Question 1:   **Luke 12:25:**
But who of you by worrying can add a single hour to his life?

Question 2:   **Proverbs 12:25a**
An anxious heart weighs a man down....

Question 3:   **Matthew 6:34a**
Therefore do not worry about tomorrow, for tomorrow will worry about itself.

Question 6:   **Matthew 11:28-30**
Come to me, all you who are weary and burdened, and I will give you rest. Take my yoke upon you and learn from me, for I am gentle and humble in heart, and you will find rest for your souls. For my yoke is easy and my burden is light.

Question 7:   **Jeremiah 31:25**
I will refresh the weary and satisfy the faint.

Psalm 104:13b
...the earth is satisfied by the fruit of his work.

Psalm 145:16
You open your hand and satisfy the desires of every living thing.

Isaiah 58:11
The Lord will guide you always; he will satisfy your needs in a sun-scorched land and will strengthen your frame. You will be like a well-watered garden, like a spring whose waters never fail.

CHAPTER 10

Question 1:   **Psalm 29:11**
The Lord gives strength to his people; the Lord blesses his people with peace.

Question 2:   **Isaiah 54:10**
"Though the mountains be shaken and the hills be removed, yet my unfailing love for you will not be shaken nor my covenant of peace be removed," says the Lord, who has compassion on you.

Question 3:   **Job 12:10**
In his hand is the life of every creature, and the breath of all mankind.

Question 4:   **1 John 4:19**
We love because he first loved us.

Question 5:   **Ephesians 4:2**
Be completely humble and gentle; be patient, bearing with one another in love.

Question 7:   **Luke 6:27**
                Love your enemies, do good to those who hate you, bless
                those who curse you, pray for those who mistreat you.

Question 10:   **Luke 6:38**
                Give, and it will be given to you. A good measure, pressed
                down, shaken together and running over, will be poured
                into your lap.

My job is to wait and see - literally to wait for the Spirit, with the Spirit, and to see.

Luci Shaw

Cindee Snider Re

Cindee is married to Tony, the man she loves most in this world, they are parents of five, ages 16-24. She and four of her five kids have Ehlers-Danlos, a genetic connective tissue disorder, and myriad co-existing conditions. While a life steeped in illness isn't what Cindee would have chosen, she also wouldn't have wanted to miss it, for she's learning that the deeper the valley, the greater her capacity for joy, for it's there, sewn into every hard, beautiful, precious moment.

Cindee is co-founder of Chronic Joy Ministry, Inc., author of the Chronic Joy Thrive Series and a passionate photographer. She and her family live in Sussex, Wisconsin, on an acre of towering pines, sugar maples and sprawling white oak that is also home to whitetail deer, wild turkey, red fox, sandhill cranes and a symphony of songbirds. Her passions include poetry, photography, research and tea. Luci Shaw is an all-time favorite poet, the Canon 100mm macro, her favorite lens (though the 85mm f1.2 is a close second), and though she frequently forgets to eat, she is never without a cup, glass or bottle of her favorite Earl Gray tea. She also serves as a patient representative on several medical grant boards.

Cindee's writing inspires readers to dig deeper, lean harder and breathe deeply of God's amazing grace.

Author Photo: Courtesy of Babboni Photography

Acknowledgments

To the *Finding Purpose Feedback Team*: **Rebecca Anne Aarup, Anne Atherton, Michelle Lee Bischoff, Mary Casey, Lisa Howard Colpo, Dee Dawson, Jean B. Ellison, Vicki Fitzsimmons, Sally Flynn, Bettie Gilbert, Kelly Greer, Anna Johnson, Heather MacLaren Johnson, Sandie Lovrien, Jamie Guerino Madeline, Diane Shrauger McElwain, Heidi Peterson, Pamela Piquette, Rachel Thiel, Jennifer Thomas-Raddatz, Gina Giordano Weeks, Gale Wilkinson** and **Jan VanKooten**, thank you for your insightful feedback, comments and questions.

Thank you to my dear friend and co-founder, **Pamela Piquette**, for praying with and for me as I wrote and for keeping me on track. Discovering Hope and Finding Purpose wouldn't exist without you.

Thank you to **Heather MacLaren Johnson, Todd Johnson, Mary Juneau, Mike Juneau, Heidi Peterson, Julie Sheridan Smith** and **Rachel Thiel**, the Board of Chronic Joy Ministry, Inc., for patiently encouraging me as I completed the manuscript for Finding Purpose. I am honored to serve with you.

A deep and personal thank you to **Megan Willome** for writing the Foreword. I cherish your words on dark days. You are a blessing!

Thank you to **Joy Lenton** for graciously consenting to the publication of your beautiful words on page 14. Poetry is the music of my soul. I am honored that you said, "Yes."

To **Max Ramsey**, "Thank you" seems insufficient. You have spoken into my life in ways you will likely never know this side of heaven.

Thank you to my parents, **Don and Susie Snider**, for your generous support of Chronic Joy Ministry, Inc., and of our first book, Discovering Hope. So much of what we do is possible because of you.

Thank you to **Wayde Peronto** of **Babboni Photography** for the gift of my author photo, possible because of **Shelly Esser**'s incredible four page interview of Pamela and I for **Just Between Us Magazine**, Summer, 2017 edition.

Thank you to my five world-shaking creatives — **Kyle, Sam, Sarah, Anna and Megan** — for the freedom to share your stories. You inspire me every single day. Thank you for believing these words have value and for encouraging me in the work of Chronic Joy.

To the man I love most in this world, my husband **Tony**, thank you for believing in me, encouraging me, praying with me and generously supporting the work of Chronic Joy. I love you!

My greatest thank you is reserved for my **Heavenly Father**. You are the breath in my lungs and the reason that I write.

And to each person reading this book: These words are a part of my life's purpose. I pray you will see God in them and that through them you will rediscover your own vital and eternal purpose.

Remember that nothing is small in the eyes of God.
Do all that you do with love.

Saint Therese of Lisieux

Discovering Hope

Beginning the Journey Toward Hope in Chronic Illness

Discovering Hope is an invitation to experience radical hope and compassionate change in a life with chronic illness. No matter how dark the days, how wild the storm, how deep the valley or how long the winter, there is hope.

There is always hope.

Discovering Hope is a powerful, practical, insightful and well-written guide for all those affected by chronic physical and mental illness.

Embrace a new perspective. Celebrate the small victories. Wrestle with difficult questions. And learn to laugh again. Often.

No matter what today looks like, there is hope.

Embracing Worth

Understanding Your Value in a Life with Chronic Illness

You are valued, sustained, beloved.

RELEASING IN 2018

Grace, Truth & Time
Facilitating Small Groups That Thrive

This valuable guide is chock-full of resources designed to empower even the most hesitant leader to become a confident, thoughtful and well-prepared facilitator.

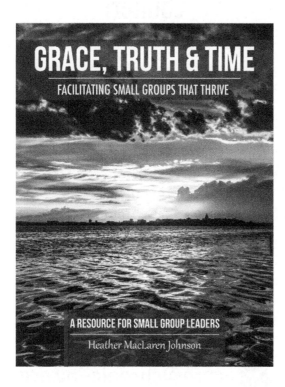

Learn to lead through God's grace; to create a space for spiritual growth and healing; to empathize, listen and engage with those in pain; to grow in prayer and compassion; to foster hope and encouragement; and to build thriving small group communities. If you've ever wondered or even doubted if you could lead a thriving chronic illness small group, this book is for you.

Connect

chronic-joy.org

cjministry

chronicjoymin

chronicjoy

chronicjoyministry

care@chronic-joy.org

WE VALUE YOUR FEEDBACK.

care@chronic-joy.org

Made in the USA
Middletown, DE
01 December 2022

16597476R00091